The Fruit of the Spirit

Galatians 5:22–23 for Children

Written by Erik Rottmann

Illustrated by Amy Huntington

CONCORDIA PUBLISHING HOUSE • SAINT LOUIS

An apple seed stuck in the ground
Will grow in branch and root
And soon, between its leaves of green,
The tree will give you fruit.

When your Lord Jesus baptized you,
His Word was sown like seed.
This seed will root and up will shoot
Good works of word and deed.

The Holy Spirit grows this seed.
He makes it leaf and sprout.
He tends to weeds and other needs
That crop up round about.

The fruit that grows from Jesus Christ
Is patience, joy, and love.
It's faithfulness and gentleness
Empowered by God above.

Goodness, peace, and self-control
Are parts of this fruit too.
Your kindness grows and soon will show
To others near to you.

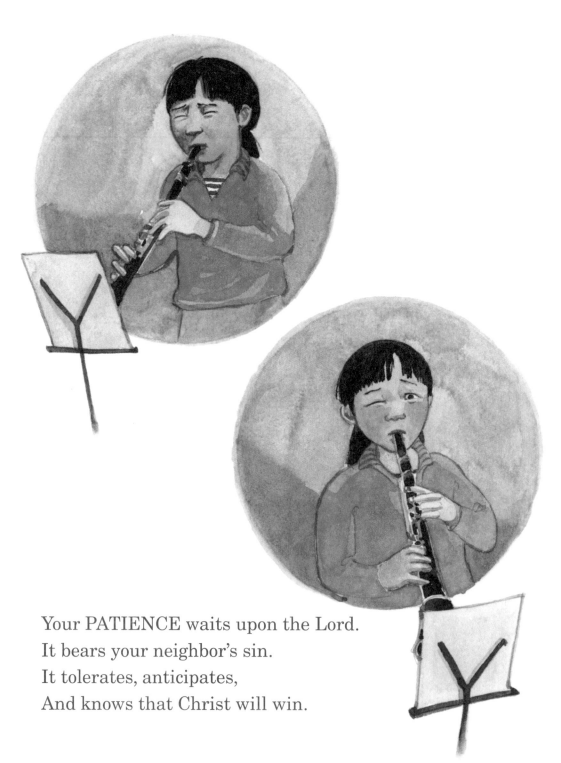

Your PATIENCE waits upon the Lord.
It bears your neighbor's sin.
It tolerates, anticipates,
And knows that Christ will win.

Your JOY is more than happiness
For things that have gone well.
JOY is the thrill that Christ has killed
Your sin and death and hell.

LOVE! Oh, LOVE! The very word
Speaks all about your Christ.
Now LOVE is yours. Through you it pours
To others in your life.

By FAITHFULNESS you take to heart
What God says in His Word.
He shall stay true. You stay here too,
Because of what you've heard.

Dear Jesus acts with GENTLENESS
Toward you, His precious child.
He'll gently do good things through you,
Through actions meek and mild.

Your GOODNESS is a treasure too.
It came to you by grace.
It sets your heart toward kindly art.
It grows with love and faith.

The way you get along with friends
Is not your greatest PEACE:
True PEACE within came when your sin
By Jesus was released!

God's gift of SELF-CONTROL gives strength
For you to face each day.
It holds your tongue when wrong is done
Or you don't get your way.

God's KINDNESS speaks a caring word
Through your own mouth and tongue.
By KINDNESS bright, Christ shines His light
Through you to everyone.

It's true this fruit won't always shine
With perfect clarity.
We each have sin that stays within.
It troubles you and me.

But even when you fall in sin,
Your Lord's deep love keeps root.
Forgiven sin and faith within
Will still produce good fruit!

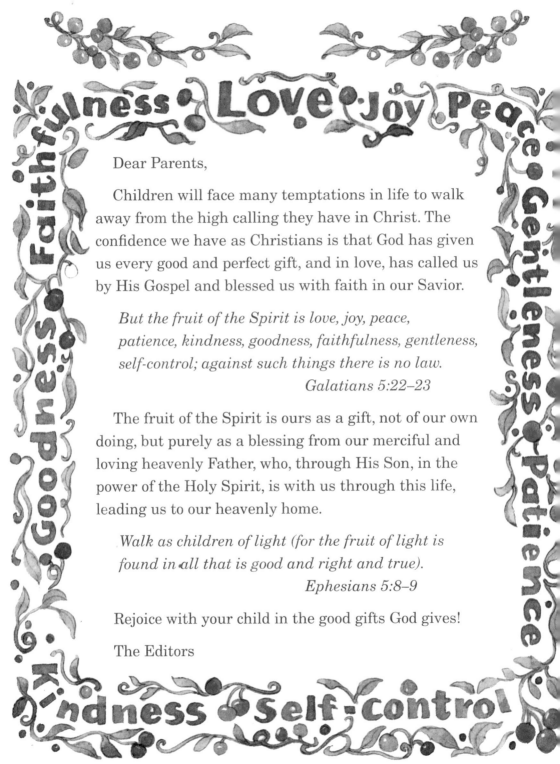

Dear Parents,

Children will face many temptations in life to walk away from the high calling they have in Christ. The confidence we have as Christians is that God has given us every good and perfect gift, and in love, has called us by His Gospel and blessed us with faith in our Savior.

But the fruit of the Spirit is love, joy, peace, patience, kindness, goodness, faithfulness, gentleness, self-control; against such things there is no law.
Galatians 5:22–23

The fruit of the Spirit is ours as a gift, not of our own doing, but purely as a blessing from our merciful and loving heavenly Father, who, through His Son, in the power of the Holy Spirit, is with us through this life, leading us to our heavenly home.

Walk as children of light (for the fruit of light is found in all that is good and right and true).
Ephesians 5:8–9

Rejoice with your child in the good gifts God gives!

The Editors